CHOLESTEROL MYTH:

The Real Truth about Cholesterol They Don't Want You to Know. Exposing the Global Conspiracy about Statins, Sugar, Supplements and Heart Disease

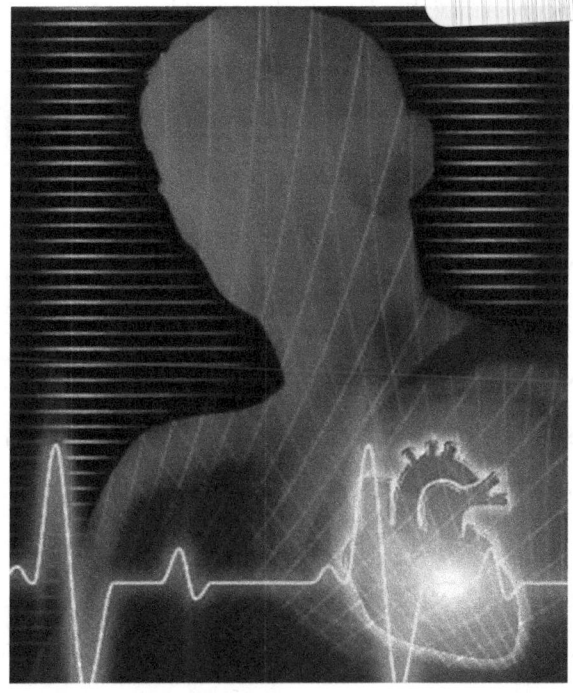

By

Joshua Collins

Table of Contents

Table of Contents 02
Foreword 04
Introduction 06
So How and When Did the Cholesterol Myth Start? 08
What is Cholesterol? 10
    The Lipoproteins – Friends or Foes 12
    Type B LDL May Be the True Culprit in Heart Disease 14
Cholesterol Numbers – What Do They Really Mean? 15
    Total Cholesterol Levels and the Incidence of Heart Attacks 15
    The importance of the Cholesterol Ratio 16
    Here's a rundown of the recommended LDL cholesterol levels by the AHA: 16
    The HDL/ Cholesterol ratio 17
    The Triglyceride/ HDL ratio 18
Triglycerides And Your Health 19
Inflammation And It's Relation to Heart Disease 21
    CRP and Homocysteine: Predictors of heart disease 23
Sugars – Are They Destroying Your Health? 27
Fructose (simple sugar) and Its Negative Effect on Your Health 31
    Fructose and Obesity 31
    Fructose and Cholesterol Levels 32
    Fructose and Diabetes 32
Lowering Cholesterol with Coconut Oil 33
What If Your Cholesterol Levels Are Too Low? 35
Why Statin Drugs Are Dangerous To Your Health 36

- Cholesterol-Lowering Supplements 39
  - Guggul 39
  - Red Rice Yeast 40
  - Policosanol 40
  - Artichoke extract 41
  - Omega 3 Fish Oil 41
  - Beta-sitosterol 42
  - Vitamin B3 (Niacin) 42
  - Soluble Fiber 42
  - Garlic extract 43
  - Ground flaxseed 43
- Smoothies to Lower Your Cholesterol 44
  - Blueberry-Avocado Smoothie 44
  - Super Chocolate Smoothie with Chia Seeds 46
  - Heart-Smart Smoothie 47
  - Green Smoothie 48
  - Orange Smoothie 49
- The Food You Eat and Cholesterol 50
  - Foods That Increase Cholesterol Levels 50
  - Foods That Lower Cholesterol Levels 52
- Exercise and Cholesterol 55
- Conclusion 57
- Recommended Reads 58
- Other Health Related Books by Joshua Collins 59
- Medical Disclaimer 60
- Copyright 61

Foreword

By Dr. Rick Levine

Having been a health care provider for over 25 years I am always searching for information that I can be share with my patients which can have an impact on their health. I am a Chiropractor who utilizes nutrition as well as other holistic, natural therapies extensively in my practice. Recently I came across an author named Joshua Collins whose work is informative, sometimes controversial, and always beneficial. He writes with passion and is an advocate of the promotion of healthier lifestyles that can be implemented by anyone seeking to improve their current health status.

Joshua Collins is a wellness expert who has extensive knowledge in the fields of nutrition, exercise and the mind-body connection. He shares his passion for helping others reach their health goals.

Joshua believes in viewing and treating the body as a whole. He understands that each person is unique in relation to their genetics, biochemistry, and psychological makeup. He understands that an individual's lifestyle choices and environmental factors can have a huge impact on their health potential.

Joshua is a proponent of a holistic medical approach that focuses on identifying the root causes of disease rather than treating just the symptoms. He believes you must first understand the origins of chronic disease prior to the development of a meaningful treatment and preventive program for an individual.

He strives to help others improve their health by providing innovative, state of the art, health tips and information. Joshua also does extensive research on many health topics and brings you information that is not "sugar coated" and sometimes his research exposes myths and misinformation that has been propagated for many years by the media and health establishment. He hopes to encourage you to make life-style changes that will both restore your health and ultimately help to prevent the onset of debilitating and life-threatening chronic diseases.

In his newest book "cholesterol Myth" he will introduce you to the world of "Big Pharma", the processed food industry and the political machine that has pulled off one of the biggest scientific misconceptions known to man. Joshua will expose the truth about cholesterol, the real indicators of heart disease and treatment options that will help you in your journey back to health.

For those who are interested in stabilizing and improving their health I recommend you read the books authored by Joshua Collins. At the very least, you will learn something new. I believe that if you implement some of the lifestyle changes recommended in his books you will also improve your health. After all without our health we are not living up to our full potential.

Dr. Rick Levine a suburban Philadelphia Chiropractor and Nutritionist who has been educating and helping people restore their health for 25+ years.

Introduction

I would say it is a good bet that you have been bombarded with confusing, facts and misinformation about cholesterol. You probably have been programmed to believe that cholesterol is bad. Am I right? We all have been led to believe that in order to live a long and healthy life one of the keys is to control our cholesterol levels. The assumption being that the less cholesterol we have in our systems the better off we will be from a health standpoint. I am here to tell you that nothing could be further from the truth.

How many times have you heard or read that you should be on a low-fat diet and should avoid high cholesterol foods like the plague? How many times have you heard that if you want to lose weight you should follow a low-fat or no fat diet? We are led to believe that if you eat too much food containing saturated fats the levels of cholesterol will rise in your body. Have you been told that ultimately the excess fats in your blood will be deposited in your arteries and result in either a heart attack or a stroke?

In reality consuming a diet that is void of fat can and will be harmful to your health. Did you know that the processed foods, additives and artificial ingredients that commonly replace wholesome nutritious foods in our diets are the real culprit in heart attacks and strokes? These synthetic ingredients and food products such as trans-fats, refined sugars, and processed grains produce chronic inflammation in our systems and that is the primary cause of disease. Cholesterol is not only an essential component of our bodies it is a building block of every cell. It is required for many of the metabolic processes that occur in our bodies and is particularly important in the production of nerve tissue, bile and certain hormones.

One of my goals in writing this book is to educate you about cholesterol numbers and how they are in and of themselves just that numbers. You will learn about cholesterol ratios and other tests which are better predictors of heart disease. I will discuss the most important cause of heart disease which is inflammation. You will learn the dangers of taking statin drugs and natural alternatives to help keep your cholesterol in check. We will also take a look at sugars and how they destroy your health and their link to high cholesterol levels.

The world of modern medicine is often filled with myths, lies and deceptions that are propagated and often funded by "Big Pharma" (pharmaceutical companies) and the processed food industry. One of the biggest medical myths is that elevated cholesterol levels are bad for you and that you have to take toxic drugs in order to lower your cholesterol levels, or you will have a heart attack or some other disastrous health event. This myth is the probably the greatest scientific deception of this century, perhaps of any century.

The research available on cholesterol is very controversial and often conflicting. I wrote this book because of the conflicting information and I know deep down in my heart that your health depends on knowing the truth. Is all the information we have been spoon fed from the media and our health care system a myth? You deserve to know the truth about cholesterol. This eBook will expose the truth about cholesterol and its role in keeping your body functioning normally.

So How and When Did the Cholesterol Myth Start?

The myth actually started in the 1960's when a very small percentage of individuals in the medical profession were claiming that cholesterol may play a part in the increased incidence of heart disease. Prior to the 60's it was common practice to ignore cholesterol levels unless it exceeded 300mg/dl.

As time passed more and more professionals jumped on the band wagon and the anti-cholesterol movement became virtually impossible to ignore. The medically accepted levels of cholesterol were lowered and from that point forward anything above 250 mg/dl was considered to be a problem. The medical profession also started to instruct people that eating too many eggs or meats was responsible for the increased incidence of heart disease.

It is interesting to note that it was the processed food industry which was leading the way in spearheading the anti-cholesterol movement and not the medical doctors. In particular it was the seed oil industry which led the way. Leading the assault on cholesterol was Archer Daniels Midland, a company that transformed crops such as corn, oilseeds, wheat and cocoa into food, feed, and agriculturally derived fuels and chemicals.

The propaganda increased and the assault on saturated fats and oils, such as coconut and palm oils, continued. They were at one point banned from importation. Then along came margarine, a butter alternative, which was promoted as a life saver. It was thought that margarine would save our nation from the increasing incidence of cardiovascular disease. It was during this time period that saturated fat was declared the villain and the main cause of heart disease and strokes.

Billions of dollars were spent by the processed food industry touting the role of cholesterol in the alarming rise of heart disease. What is interesting though is that "Big Pharma" to this point had basically ignored this propaganda about the perceived correlation between cholesterol and cardiovascular disease.

Everything changed in the mid to late 1970's when statin drugs were developed. Now the pharmaceutical establishment anointed cholesterol as the main culprit in the development of cardiovascular disease. Statin drugs were now looked upon as the "medicinal savior" of our modern society. This all-out war against cholesterol continues today evidenced by the American Heart Association's recommendation that the total cholesterol ideally should be less than 200 milligrams per deciliter. Back in 2004 the AHA also lowered the suggested ideal levels of LDL from 130 to less than 100 and recommended for patients who are at high-risk, that their LDL levels should be lower than 70 mg/dl.

What is Cholesterol?

You might be asking yourself what the heck is cholesterol and why is it so important? Physically, it is a waxy, fat-like material found in all of the cells in the body. The body is, on its own, capable of manufacturing the cholesterol that it needs on a daily basis to build cells and maintain various aspects of normal physiology. Our bodies need cholesterol to create hormones, vitamin D, and other substances that help digest the foods that we eat. Cholesterol is also found in various food products that we consume such as meats and certain oils.

A leading anti-aging doctor in the United States, Dr. Ron Rosedale, explained that there is actually just one type of cholesterol. Cholesterol is just cholesterol. Because our watery blood and fat do not mix well, it has to be combined with proteins and other fats in order to be carried in the bloodstream properly. It is the combination of plain old cholesterol with a carrier protein that has been classified as HDL (high density lipoprotein) and LDL (low density lipoprotein) and VLDL (very low density lipoprotein).

Cholesterol is needed by the body to produce vitamin D. The best way to maintain adequate levels of vitamin D is by exposing oneself safely to the sun. The UVB rays found in sunlight interacts with the cholesterol in the skin which aids in the manufacture of vitamin D. If your cholesterol level is too low, you will not be able to generate vitamin D effectively, no matter how much you expose yourself to the sun.

Cholesterol is not bad, despite what we are led to believe. We have been programed to believe that it is the culprit behind cardiac and circulatory problems, but that is not entirely the case. It is an important component of every cell membrane found here on Earth. It has been found that lowering one's cholesterol levels too much could actually lead to death. Vital hormones are made with the help of cholesterol. Without it, hormones cannot be produced effectively.

Cholesterol travels in the body through the bloodstream in small packs known as lipoproteins. These substances consist of an external protein layer and a fat (or lipid) internally. There are three main types of lipoproteins that carry cholesterol in the body: the high-density lipoproteins (HDL), low-density lipoproteins (LDL), and very low-density lipoproteins (VLDL). It is important to have healthy levels of these lipoproteins in the body at all times.

LDL cholesterol is often referred to as the bad type of cholesterol. High levels of low-density lipoproteins have been implicated in the build-up of cholesterol in the arteries, which could then lead to the onset of various cardiac and circulatory problems.

HDL cholesterol is often referred to as the good type of cholesterol. HDL or High Density Lipoprotein is a specific type of lipoprotein whose main function is to carry cholesterol from different parts of the body back to the liver. The liver then recycles the cholesterol and re-packages it with protein particles which are then delivered to the cells and tissues as needed. The body always tries to conserve and make cholesterol because it is constantly needed to keep the body functioning at its peak physiological level.

The Lipoproteins – Friends or Foes

Cholesterol is actually not bad. It is considered an essential fat that helps support the membranes of practically every cell in the body. Some of the cholesterol used in the body comes from a person's diet while additional cholesterol is produced by the liver. Cholesterol is not normally dissolved in the blood, so special proteins called lipoproteins are necessary to carry it to where it needs to go.

This lipoprotein carrier system actually acts like a microscopic group of buses that house and carries cholesterol through the blood stream. Each type of lipoprotein has a different density and each also behaves quite differently than the other types. There are three main types of lipoproteins, the low-density lipoproteins (LDL), high-density lipoproteins (HDL) and very low-density lipoproteins (VLDL).

A particle of LDL consists of a cholesterol center with an outer covering of lipoprotein. These particles are considered low-density because they are less dense than other cholesterol particles. LDL is considered to be the "bad" type of cholesterol. This is due to its chemical makeup and the fact that LDL cholesterol in the bloodstream, under the proper circumstances, could lead to the formation of plaques along the arterial walls and ultimately atherosclerosis.

I know I promised not to give you a chemistry lesson however it is necessary to give you a watered down one here. LDL in and of itself is not bad. It is the levels of oxidized LDL which has been identified as a major issue. I know your next question is "What in the world is oxidation?" We have all witnessed a freshly-cut apple that quickly turns brown, a bicycle fender that becomes rusty over time, and a copper penny suddenly turns green. What do all of these events have in common? They are all examples of a process called oxidation. This process occurs when oxygen molecules interacts with another substance. It is defined as the loss of at least one electron when two or more substances interact. Your next question might be "where does oxidized LDL come from?" It comes from artificial, partially hydrogenated oils (trans-fats), vegetable oils, and genetically modified food, a diet high in refined sugars, alcohol and tobacco. It is also found in in meats and fats that have been heated to very high temperatures in frying and other high-temperature processes.

HDL is considered to be the "good" type of cholesterol. High-density lipoproteins are actually the smallest of all lipoproteins in the body. HDLs are needed for lipid metabolism and they support the immune system in parasitic attacks and inflammation. HDL is primarily produced in the body by the liver and the intestines. HDL acts somewhat like a scavenger for cholesterol. This cholesterol works by transporting damaging low-density lipoprotein and very-low-density lipoprotein to your liver, where they are broken down, allowing your body to eliminate them. It keeps cholesterol away from the arteries in the body, and it also removes excess cholesterol from any plaque build-up. These cholesterol particles are extremely helpful in preventing the onset of heart disease.

Very low-density lipoproteins (VLDL) are a form of cholesterol that helps to distribute triglycerides through the bloodstream. A portion of this type of cholesterol also converts into low-density lipoprotein (LDL). The major difference between LDL and VLDL is that the percentage of protein in the VLDL is much lower and the percentages of triglycerides are much higher in VLDL when compared to LDL. Triglycerides are mainly used for energy production. VLDL is the body's main source of energy during continuous prolonged fasting. Triglycerides are stored as fat cells and released for energy between meals and when more calories are burned than consumed.

To sum it up LDL contains the highest amount of cholesterol. HDL contains the highest amount of protein. VLDL contains the highest amount of triglyceride, a blood fat.

Type B LDL May Be the True Culprit in Heart Disease

There is a sub-group of LDL called type B LDL and is considered to be the main culprit when it comes to heart disease. The type B lipoproteins are composed of a compound called Apo lipoprotein B (ApoB). High levels of Apo lipoprotein B in the body have been found to lead to the formation of plaques and contribute to cardiovascular disease.

Cholesterol Numbers – What Do They Really Mean?

You might be wondering, what is the correlation between cholesterol levels and a person's health. More importantly you should be asking yourself whether or not there is a correlation between high cholesterol levels in the blood and the incidence of heart disease or strokes. There are many individuals who say that total cholesterol numbers are to blame for the onset of various health problems, such as cardiac or circulatory problems. However, there have been numerous studies conducted that have shown otherwise.

Total Cholesterol Levels and the Incidence of Heart Attacks

To date, heart disease tops the list of diseases that kill Americans. During the beginning of the 20th century, heart disease was relatively uncommon. More and more people are developing and suffering from heart disease each and every year, and it has been found that the preventative measures being taken by medical professionals and their patients are not enough. It is important to address the underlying cause of heart disease, which is the decrease of blood flow into the heart initiated by an inflammatory reaction in the arteries.

Various studies have shown that it takes more than just simply lowering one's cholesterol levels in order to protect oneself from heart disease. A national study conducted recently has shown that about 75% of the patients who had been hospitalized due to a heart attack had cholesterol levels that were not in the high risk category for a cardiovascular problem. The numbers in these studies were compared with the national cholesterol guidelines. In another study, 50% of people who had heart attacks had normal cholesterol levels. It has been theorized that elevated cholesterol levels are not the real cause of heart disease and it is inflammation within our arteries is the real culprit and that cholesterol attaches to it in an effort to repair the inflamed artery.

The importance of the Cholesterol Ratio

In the United States, health officials encourage everyone age 20 and up to have their cholesterol levels checked at least one time every 5 years. Testing will determine the total sum of cholesterol present in your blood, the HDL, LDL, and indirectly the VLDL (very low-density lipoprotein). According to the American heart Association, the total cholesterol ideally should be less than 200 milligrams per deciliter (mg/dl). At one point in time, it should be noted, medical practitioners were not concerned with cholesterol levels unless the readings were above 300 but over the years the recommended levels have drastically changed.

The American Heart Association (AHA) updated their guidelines for cholesterol levels back in 2004, which lowered the suggested ideal levels of LDL from 130 to less than 100. For patients who are at high-risk, they recommend that they should have LDL levels lower than 70 mg/dl.

Here's a rundown of the recommended LDL cholesterol levels by the AHA:

- An LDL level of less than 100 mg/dL is considered optimal.
- An LDL of 100 up to 129 mg/dL is considered near-optimal.
- An LDL level between 130 and 159 is borderline high.
- An LDL level of 160 to 189 mg/dL is considered high.
- An LDL level of 190 or more is very high.

Here's a rundown of recommended HDL levels by the AHA:

- An HDL level less than 40 mg/dl for men and less than 50 mg/dl for women is considered a major risk
- An HDL level 60 mg/dl or higher is considered protective

Because of the above guidelines, doctors give their patients different drugs that aim to lower the cholesterol levels. However, there have been numerous cases wherein individuals who had total cholesterol levels higher than 250 mg/dl were actually at a low risk for heart disease due to their above average HDL levels. There are also people who were at very high risk even when they had cholesterol levels below 200.

The ability to predict if you are at a risk for heart disease is better served by looking at the following two ratios:

- HDL/ Cholesterol ratio
- Triglyceride/ HDL ratio

The HDL/ Cholesterol ratio

Your HDL/cholesterol ratio is actually a very effective measure to predict your risk factor of heart disease. You can check this by dividing your HDL level by your cholesterol level. The resulting ratio should be above 24%.

The Triglyceride/ HDL ratio

The triglyceride to HDL ratio is also a better predictor of heart disease than looking at total cholesterol levels, HDL and LDL individually.

The result ideally should be below 2. However, you have to remember that these are simply guidelines. There are a lot of other factors that increase one's risk of developing heart disease. Just looking at the total cholesterol is a poor indicator of one's risk. HDL and LDL levels individually can give you a peek of what is going on in your body, but they do not necessarily show you everything that you need to know.

Triglycerides And Your Health

A discussion of cholesterol would not be complete without talking about triglycerides. Just like cholesterol the food we eat is one of the sources of triglycerides. Our liver also produces them especially when you consume high caloric meals that are filled with carbohydrates. Excess carbohydrates which are ingested end up getting stored in fat cells. When your body needs an alternative source of energy they get released from fat storage as fatty acids which fuel the body and provide energy for bodily processes.

If you are wondering where and why your triglycerides are high just pull out a few products from your refrigerator and take a look at the labels. There is a good chance that you will see as one of the ingredients high fructose corn syrup (HFCS). HFCS has been linked in many scientific studies to increase levels of triglycerides. In animal studies in addition to the elevated triglycerides there was also weight gain especially related to abdominal fat. When you look at humans the deadly combination of elevated triglyceride levels and increased abdominal fat has been correlated with not only type 2 diabetes but also heart disease.

Elevated triglycerides are commonly associated with a set of metabolic disturbances which include increased LDL levels, decreased HDL levels, increased abdominal fat, insulin resistance, hypertension and adult onset diabetes (type 2 diabetes). This combination of metabolic imbalances has been coined "Syndrome X". It is estimate that about 25% to 35% of the US population exhibits the findings in Syndrome X.

Below is a list of the recommended levels of triglycerides by the National Cholesterol Education Program:

Normal	less than 150 mg/dl
Borderline High	150-199 mg/dl
High	200-499 mg/dl
Very High	500 mg/dl or higher

Just like elevated cholesterol levels high triglycerides has been treated medically with statin drugs (see chapter on Statins for more information). Niacin is one of the least expensive and probably the most effective overall treatment for both lowering cholesterol and triglycerides. Treatment should be started with a baseline dose of no more than 250 mg per day. The dosage can be increased to levels between 1000 and 3000 mg/day as long as you can tolerate the most common side effect which is flushing. As with any treatment whether natural or chemical you should be under the care of a professional who can monitor your program.

To summarize a diet consisting of excessive amounts of simple sugars (sucrose and HFCS) stimulate the liver to synthesize fat which get converted to triglycerides which get stored in tissues of our bodies. Fats ingested via our diet also contribute to elevated blood triglyceride levels but not as much as sugar. The elevate triglyceride levels in the blood combined with the fat which accumulates in our bodies leads to insulin resistance. Insulin resistance simply means our bodies no longer respond effectively to insulin which leads to elevated blood sugars and the onset of type 2 diabetes. The most effective treatment is to reduce the intake of simple sugars like HFCS and sucrose. When you add this to an effective exercise program and the resulting weight loss there is a good chance your triglyceride and blood sugar levels will return to normal.

Inflammation And It's Relation to Heart Disease

The process of inflammation is actually the body's own attempt to protect itself and repair damaged tissues in the body. The inflammatory reaction is designed to remove any harmful stimuli, such as pathogens, irritants, and damaged cells from the body. The inflammatory reaction initiates the healing process within our bodies. This reaction is part of the "normal" immune response within the body. However there are instances when inflammation can trigger a "snowball effect" whereby inflammation increases and increases to the detriment of the body. This is the exact process that occurs in atherosclerosis and the formation of plaques within the arteries.

From a medical standpoint inflammation is an indicator of many disease processes, including heart disease. We have been lead to believe that heart disease is caused by elevated cholesterol levels even though there is evidence that suggests that heart disease results from inflammation in the coronary arteries. It is important to understand the role of inflammation in the body to better understand how inflammation actually acts as a better predictor of heart disease.

Inflammation is a natural response of the body to various invaders and damaged tissues. During inflammation blood vessels constrict to wall off the area to prevent further damage. Blood cells known as platelets are jettisoned to the area and a clot forms which acts as a natural band aid covering the inflamed tissues. The immune system then sends various chemicals and cells to neutralize the damaged cells and initiate the repair of damaged cells. In the arterial walls this process and the resulting band aid is known as "arterial plaque". When the arteries become inflamed, the risk of suffering a heart attack increases dramatically.

In looking at the preceding explanation of inflammation you should notice that cholesterol was not even in the picture. Cholesterol only comes to play because it is needed to help replace or repair the damaged cells. The liver is prompted to produce more cholesterol which is then released into your blood stream because of the presence of the damaged cells. This is a process that is deliberate because it is needed to produce healthy cells. You may not know it, but it is possible that microscopic damage may be occurring within the body on a regular basis. Because of this, your body may actually be in a state of chronic inflammation, which is dangerous.

So elevated cholesterol levels is not really the problem, it is merely the solution your body is using to try and heal itself. Inflammation in the arterial walls is the real danger, and if left unchecked the swelling can eventually shut off blood flow to the heart or brain, which can cause a heart attack or stroke.

Some of the common causes of chronic inflammation in the body are a diet high in sugar/fructose, smoking, eating a diet full of nutrient deficient processed foods, chronic stress and yes lack of exercise.

CRP and Homocysteine: Predictors of heart disease

C Reactive Protein (CRP)

There is a test used to determine if a person suffers from chronic inflammation within the body. The test is known as the C-reactive protein blood test (CRP). The CRP level is used as an indicator if a person suffers from any inflammation in the body including that which occurs in arteries. Here's a rundown of the different CRP results that are helpful in predicting the risk of inflammation resulting in heart disease:

- Levels under 1 milligram per liter of blood indicates a low risk for cardiovascular disease.

- A level between 1 to 3 milligrams means you have an intermediate risk.

- Levels more than 3 milligrams indicate a high risk.

Homocysteine

In the war against the "almighty Cholesterol", the high levels of a substance called homocysteine are often forgotten. Homocysteineis an amino acid, and it has been positively correlated with the buildup plaque in the arteries and the tendency to form clots which is a deadly combination. Normal levels of homocysteine in the blood are Below 17 micromoles/L. In an ideal situation you should aim at keeping the levels below 8.0 micromoles/L.

Nutrients that lower homocysteine levels are folic acid, vitamins B6 and B12 and choline which are found mostly in animal foods. In a study conducted in the Netherlands the conclusion was that daily supplementation with 5 mg of folic acid, 0.4mg of hydroxycobalamin (Vitamin B12), and 50 mg of pyridoxine (Vitamin B6) reduces homocysteine levels in patients with venous thrombosis (clotting) as well as in healthy control subjects.

To date, conventional medicine is slowly warming up to the idea that heart attacks and cardiovascular disease may be better correlated with chronic inflammation in the body as opposed to solely blaming cholesterol levels to be main player in these diseases. However, the majority of medical practitioners still see increased cholesterol levels as the cause of heart disease and heart attacks, and not the underlying damage found in the arteries.

Having increased levels of cholesterol in the blood may be attributed to the increased inflammation in the body but not in a negative way. The cholesterol in the blood is actually there in order to do its job: to help the body repair and heal from any damage received. Traditional medical practitioners still tell us that cholesterol should be lowered using various drugs because this will help reduce one's risk of heart attacks.

However, in the previous discussions, it has been noted that numerous studies have been conducted showing that cholesterol levels are not directly correlated with one's risk of developing heart disease and heart attacks. We are missing the fact that whatever is causing the inflammatory reaction should be stopped and we should not simply focus on the elevated levels of cholesterol. What has been forgotten is the normal role of cholesterol in the body and instead it has been anointed the main culprit of heart disease. A far better approach would be a plan to reduce the body's extra need to manufacture and use cholesterol, which is mainly due to the damage that is occurring inside the body from chronic inflammation.

It can be dangerous if your cholesterol levels plummet below normal. Remember that cholesterol is a building block of every cell in the body, even those found in the brain. This is why when you have low cholesterol levels your brain can also go haywire. Your brain chemistry as well as your psyche is affected by cholesterol levels that are too low.

There was a study by Dutch researchers that found men who had long-term below normal cholesterol levels actually had a higher risk of developing symptoms of depression. This is because cholesterol is also responsible for the metabolism of serotonin, which is a neurotransmitter that is involved in the regulation of one's mood. A similar research done by Canadian research group found that people who had a total cholesterol level in the lowest 25% of the ideal range were 6 times more prone of committing suicide than those who had cholesterol levels in the highest quarter. Dozens of other studies have shown the connection between lowered or low cholesterol levels and violent behavior. Lowered cholesterol levels can cause the brains serotonin activity to be lowered to an unhealthy level which could then increase the chances of aggressive and violent behavior.

An optimum level of total cholesterol is said to be 200 mg/dl, although nowadays many medical practitioners would say that it should be below 200 and the lower the better. Any level under 150 is already considered low. Levels below 150 could be harmful to the body as well as your overall health.

So when all is said and done is high serum cholesterol measurements useless? NO! It definitely indicates the presence of a metabolic imbalance and indicates that there is substantial damage in the body that requires repair.

Then what in the world are the real causes of heart attacks and strokes? The literature definitely indicates that the following parameters can have an impact on you cardiovascular health.

High triglyceride levels in the blood

Low HDL cholesterol levels

High homocysteine levels

Dietary deficiency of saturated fats and cholesterol

Overload of oxidized cholesterol containing foods (processed foods, partially hydrogenated oils (trans- fats), vegetable oils, and genetically modified food)

If you can control your triglyceride levels, increase your HDL cholesterol levels, reduce your homocysteine levels, reduced the intake of processed foods and vegetable oils, increase your intake of healthy saturated fats (coconut oil) and exercise you have the ability to reduce your likelihood of developing cardiovascular disease.

Sugars – Are They Destroying Your Health?

We will now take a look at sugar, another substance that is present in many of the foods that you eat. Sugar is digested, like all other types of carbohydrates, primarily in the intestines and the end result is the formation of glucose. Glucose is the main source of energy for cells in the body. Glucose is transported to the various parts of the body by the blood, and it is absorbed into the cells to be turned into energy. Insulin, a hormone secreted by the pancreas is ultimately responsible for controlling the uptake of glucose by the cells. A diet which is high in refined sugar can be very dangerous and literally ruin one's health.

Sugar is actually a very addictive substance, and many experts consider it as a low-grade type of poison, similar to any other substance that is addictive in nature. Most foods nowadays contain refined sugar (high fructose corn syrup and white sugar) which are basically sugars which has been stripped of their essential nutrients. It provides empty calories and does not have the natural nutrients that are present in whole sugar cane or whole sugar beet. Many people do not even know that most of the foods and drinks they are ingesting actually contain massive amounts of refined sugar. Refined sugar is considered to be an incomplete carbohydrate. The body is unable to make use of refined carbohydrates that have been stripped of vitamins, proteins, and minerals that are normally found in an unrefined complete carbohydrate.

Many people often try to eat foods with high concentrations of sugar as a way of relieving hunger or as an energy pick me up; however there have been studies that have shown that it is better to eat nothing at all than eat refined sugar. In order for the body to be able to digest, eliminate, and detoxify the body of sugar, the body tissues have to surrender vital minerals and vitamins. Due to this negative exchange, deficiencies can be triggered in the body which could ultimately cause the cells to become weak.

When cells become weak then the tissues, organs, and body systems become affected, too, resulting to poor health. When the body tries to make use of these incomplete carbohydrates, toxic substances form, such as abnormal molecules that have five carbon atoms, and pyruvic acid. When pyruvic acid accumulates in the blood, brain and nervous system serious problems arise.

Both of these toxic materials, pyruvic acid and 5 carbon atoms, interfere with the natural process of respiration of the cells in the body. The cells, with the presence of these abnormal and toxic substances are unable to get the needed amount of oxygen which is necessary for survival. The cells deprived of oxygen die off and depending on the tissue type the body may not be able to replace them. The permanent death of cells could then interfere with the normal functioning of the different parts of the body. This could then trigger the onset of degenerative diseases. It is interesting to note that cancer cells are anaerobic by nature and can exist and proliferate without the presence of oxygen.

Any kind of excess sugar present in the body if not being utilized by the cells for energy get converted into fatty acids in the liver to be used as an alternative source of energy for the cells. These fatty acids are then kept or stored and get deposited in the thighs, belly, as well as around the vital organs of the body. Because of this abnormal accumulation, the organs over time cease to function effectively. The entire body suffers because of this, and this leads to poor overall health. All sugar, especially the refined type, also makes the blood and the body tissues acidic, which is perfect for the development and the survival of various viruses, microorganisms and cancer cells. Microorganisms replicate better in an acidic environment and cancer cells multiply at a faster rate. You have to be able to keep your blood and body tissues alkaline to in order to maintain optimal health. If you have an excessive amount of sugar in your diet, you will have a difficult time of maintaining the alkalinity of your blood and body tissues and your health will suffer.

The more one eats sugar, the more one craves it. He or she is then trapped in a never-ending cycle of sugar eating and craving. Sugar cravings happen for a number of reasons such as from eating unbalanced meals that do not contain enough proteins and fats and are nutrient deficient. Eating at irregular times, skipping meals, and consuming of large quantities of sugars and sweet food also increase the level of cravings. There is also an emotional component attached to the consumption of sugar. Many attach feelings of comfort, love, and security with the eating of sweets. These feelings should be separated from the act of eating sugar.

Any emotional attachment or addiction to sugar should be worked on with the help of a medical practitioner. The addiction can be resolved by taking in nutrients that will help balance the need and craving for sugar by regulating the centers for blood sugar control. Withdrawal from sugar addiction should be done gradually while providing the body with large amounts of substances that have been depleted from the body tissues.

A famous doctor, Dr. Nancy Appleton, wrote more than a hundred reasons why sugar is the culprit to many diseases and a number of those reasons have to do with cholesterol levels. Here are some of the things she wrote regarding sugar:

- Sugar suppresses the functions of the immune system.

- Sugar can actually produce a significant increase in the triglyceride levels.

- Sugar can cause anxiety, crankiness, hyperactivity, and difficulty in concentrating among children.

- Sugar reduces the amount of high-density lipoproteins, or "good" cholesterol in the body.

- Sugar intake can lead to ovarian cancer.

- Sugar makes the digestive tract acidic.

- Sugar has been found to cause premature aging in people.

- Sugar intake can lead to the development of alcoholism.
- Sugar can cause the development of heart disease.
- Sugar can cause the formation of varicose veins.
- Sugar supports the growth of Candida Albicans, the culprit behind yeast infections
- Sugar can increase total cholesterol levels
- Sugar can increase one's risk of cardiovascular disease.
- Sugar helps in the increase of low-density lipoproteins, or the "bad" cholesterol.
- Sugar increases the amount of fat stored in the liver.
- Sugar compromises the lining of the capillaries.
- Sugar can actually trigger the onset of headaches, including migraines.

Fructose (simple sugar) and Its Negative Effect on Your Health

Fructose is a monosaccharide which is a fancy name for a simple sugar. It occurs naturally and is present in many food items including vine fruits, berries, root crops, and tree fruits. There are three forms of fructose available commercially. These are crystalline, sucrose, and HFCS or high-fructose corn syrup. Sucrose is a fancy name for table sugar which is made of two monosaccharides, fructose and glucose. Commercial-grade fructose has many uses, but the most popular one is as a sweetener in fruit juices and carbonated beverages.

Fructose is water-soluble. It is also readily absorbed by the small intestine and into the bloodstream. The consumption of this simple sugar can drastically influence the human body on many levels. Some of its effects are discussed in the succeeding paragraphs.

Fructose and Obesity

Many studies have been conducted to explore the relationship between fructose and weight gain. So far, the conclusion remains the same: these two are directly correlated. This means that individuals who consume a high amount of fructose are more likely to gain weight and eventually become obese than those with a normal to low intake of this type of simple sugar. This "fattening" effect is a direct result of the influence fructose has on the levels of ghrelin, insulin, and leptin in the body. To elaborate, in a 2007 study, it was found that the human test subjects who were asked to partake of high-fructose drinks while eating had higher ghrelin and lower insulin and leptin levels in their systems after their meal compared to the subjects who drank high-glucose beverages. Since ghrelin is known to induce appetite while the other two hormones are known appetite suppressors, it was hypothesized that fructose makes a person eat more and gain weight in the process.

Fructose and Cholesterol Levels

As with obesity/weight gain, the levels of cholesterol in the body also have a direct correlation with fructose intake. When a person consumes excessive amounts of fructose, the levels of both triglycerides and LDL cholesterol spike. High levels of triglycerides in the blood, also known as hypertriglyceridemia have been associated with a cerebrovascular accident also known as a stroke. We have spoken in length about elevated LDL cholesterol levels in other parts of this book so I will not repeat them here. Simply put, the presence of high levels of fructose in the body makes a person more at risk of suffering from cardiovascular disease – a condition that can be fatal when left unaddressed.

Fructose and Diabetes

The role of fructose in diabetes is not as clear as that in weight gain and the cholesterol levels in the human body. In fact, until now there are still doubts as to whether its consumption contributes significantly to the onset of diabetes or if there are other factors that should instead be focused on. Despite the lack of unanimity, though, most scientists and medical experts acknowledge the fact that consuming high amounts of fructose leads to insulin resistance – a condition wherein the body is unable to use insulin properly because the cells have become resistant to it. As a result, more insulin is produced by the pancreas to compensate for what the brain thinks is a shortage of the said hormone. This leads to hyperglycemia or high blood sugar – the most common symptom of diabetes mellitus.

Lowering Cholesterol with Coconut Oil

Coconut oil has long been in the crosshairs of various alternative medicine practitioners. They believe that coconut oil actually has the capacity to help lower cholesterol levels. There have been studies that have shown that the supplementation of coconut oil in the diet could actually help in the reduction of one's waist circumference, plus many other great benefits including the increase in HDL cholesterol levels and the lowering of the LDL/HDL ratios.

In a 12-week study, researchers found positive results on the waist circumference and the biochemical profiles of 40 obese women from ingesting coconut oil when compared to the effects of ingesting soybean oil. In this study half of the women took soybean oil while the other half took coconut oil. Those who took coconut oil had significant changes in their biochemical profiles and their waist circumference. They had increased levels of high-density lipoproteins and a reduced LDL/HDL ratio. The women also had a reduced waist circumference. Contrary to what you have been led to believe coconut oil is actually very good for you and can help you lose weight and improve your cholesterol profile.

Coconut oil, though it contains saturated fats, is actually considered as a rare gem that has extraordinary health benefits. Multiple studies done on people from the Pacific Islands who have about 30-60% of their total calorie intake from saturated coconut oil have been found to have almost nonexistent incidence of heart disease. Other studies have shown that dietary supplementation with coconut oil helps people improve their lipid profiles. It does not cause dyslipidemia, or a state wherein fat or cholesterol in the blood is in abnormal amounts. Coconut oil has also been found to be extremely helpful for nursing moms, those who have digestive problems, pregnant women, and even athletes. It is rich in lauric acid, which is converted into monolaurin by the body, which helps strengthen the immune system. Coincidently monolaurin is found in significant concentrations in breast milk.

Coconut oil has been found to promote healthy cholesterol levels and heart health contrary to what we have been led believe. The oil also helps balance the thyroid gland (suppression of the thyroid increases the cholesterol in the blood) which also helps normalize the cholesterol levels. The medium-chain fatty acids found in coconut oil also help raise the body's metabolism which is beneficial if you are interested in losing weight.

I have also written a comprehensive book on the benefits of Coconut Oil which is titled "**Coconut Oil Handbook: Nature's miracle for weight loss, healthy hair, and a beautiful you**!" and is available at the Kindle store on Amazon.com. This book provides a comprehensive look at the many benefits of ingesting coconut oil from both a medicinal and non-medicinal perspective.

What If Your Cholesterol Levels Are Too Low?

As I stated in a previous chapter cholesterol is essential for your body to function normally. It is involved in hormone production, vitamin D synthesis, and cell membrane stability. Bile salts, which aid in the digestion of fats in your system, are also dependent on cholesterol. We also know how important cholesterol is in normal brain and neurological function. So why in the world would you want to lower your cholesterol levels to dangerously low levels?

I recently read a research study titled "Arteriosclerosis, Thrombosis, and Vascular Biology" that indicated that low HDL cholesterol levels was very much associated with the decline in memory in middle age adults. My feeling is that rather than messing around with your brain why not nourish it with Omega 3 fatty acids which have been proven to improve brain function and normalize HDL levels.

The negative effects of having your cholesterol too low is has also been associated with depression, suicidal thoughts, violent behavioral patterns, Parkinson's disease and even some forms of cancer.

A prominent researcher at MIT, Dr. Stephanie Seneff, has been quoted as saying that "Heart disease, I think, is a cholesterol deficiency problem, and in particular cholesterol sulfate deficiency problem..." Her extensive research, has led her to the conclusion that what we call "cardiovascular disease," and the resultant arterial plaque, is actually your body's way to compensate for not having enough cholesterol sulfate available.

Why Statin Drugs Are Dangerous To Your Health

Statins are a class of drugs that are commonly prescribed my medical practitioners to help lower the levels of cholesterol in the body. These groups of drugs are able to interfere with the action of a certain chemical found in the liver that is responsible for the production of cholesterol. Several types of statin drugs are available in the market, from atorvastatin(Lipitor), lovastatin(Mevacor), fluvastatin(Lescol) rosuvastatin(Crestor), simvastatin(Zocor), and mevastatin(Compactin). Rosuvastatin and atorvastatin are considered to be the most potent, and fluvastatin is considered as the least potent. Mevastatin is a naturally-occurring type of statin that could be found in red yeast rice.

More and more experts have come to find that if your goal is to lower your cholesterol levels, taking drugs should be the last action one takes on your list of things to do. Many practitioners have seen that people do not really need the drugs to lower their cholesterol levels. A statistic showed that out of 20,000 patients in a clinic, only 4 or 5 of those patients really needed drugs for lowering cholesterol due to a genetic anomaly called familial hypercholesterolemia. It is estimated that more than half of Americans take one or more drugs that are prescribed for one or more chronic health conditions. The second most common group of individuals belongs to those who take cholesterol-lowering medications, being about 15 percent of the population.

The continuous use of statins is actually dangerous to one's health. Statins, as stated above, work by inhibiting the enzyme found in the liver that is essential for the production of cholesterol. However, if you interfere with the normal processes of the body, chances are you will be causing an imbalance in the body, which is not a good thing. Statins have been found to not only inhibit the production of essential cholesterol, but it also inhibits the production of other intermediary substances, many of which are also important for various biochemical functions in the body.

To make it even worse, statins tend to deplete the body's Coenzyme Q10 (or CoQ10) stores. This is an enzyme that is actually very good for muscle function and heart health. Doctors rarely tell the people who take statins of this, and they rarely prescribe CoQ10 supplements for their patients that do take cholesterol lowering drugs. This then leads to the depletion of CoQ10, leading to the onset of soreness, fatigue, muscle weakness, and later on, heart failure. Rhabdomyolysis, or muscle weakness and pain, is actually one the most common side effects of the use of statin drugs. This occurs because statins turn "on" the atrogin-1 gene, which plays a major role in the atrophy of muscles.

In addition, rhabdomyolysis is also an indication that the body tissues are already breaking down, which then could cause damage to the kidneys. The use of statin drugs has also been linked to the following effects:

- Dizziness
- Depression
- Increased risk of nerve damage or polyneuropathy (pain in the feet and hands)
- Impairment of the cognitive function, including loss of memory
- Liver problems, including the increase of liver enzymes
- Decreased potency of the immune system
- A potential increase in the risk for cancer development.

It has also been found recently that statins could increase one's risk of developing Lou Gehrig's disease (ALS). These drugs do in fact lower the cholesterol levels of a person, but it has not been proven that these help make those who take such drugs healthier. Statins have not been fully proven to help people become healthier and avoid heart disease.

There is a "new kid on the block" group of cholesterol lowering drug called PCSK9 Inhibitors. These newer drugs, PCSK9 inhibitors, target and suppress a particular gene involved in the regulation of how much cholesterol your liver can actually filter out. They have the potential to lower your cholesterol levels to dangerous levels in the range of 50 mg/dl. With these rock bottom levels comes the added potential of harm to your body and can in my opinion lead to health problems.

The key to preventing heart disease lies in the lowering of inflammation in the body. This could be achieved through natural means, without the harmful effects of drugs like statins.

The key to preventing heart disease is to understand and accept the fact that high levels of cholesterol indicates that there is a problem of inflammation and the associated metabolic imbalance somewhere in your system resulting in damaged cells. Whenever there are damaged cells and chronic inflammation in your body additional cholesterol is produced in an effort to repair those cells. As we discussed in the chapter on inflammation and its relation to heart disease it makes sense to identify the causes of chronic inflammation in the body and address them rather than taking a synthetic drug which can cause extensive damage to your body.

Cholesterol-Lowering Supplements

There are various supplements in the marketplace that have been found to help people restore their cholesterol to healthy levels. When combined with a sensible diet they have been found to be very effective. This section will discuss the different supplements that can help you lower and maintain your cholesterol levels at healthy levels naturally.

Guggul

Even as far back as 600 B.C., people in India have been using guggul, a gum resin, to treat various types of ailments. Guggul is originally from a tree called the Commuphoa Mukul, and it is vastly used in Ayurvedic medicine. This type medical philosophy and practice is considered to be one of the oldest known systems that make use of herbs and plants in the healing. Ayurvedic medicine also focuses on the diet. With the use of guggul, people have reported relief from the various conditions:

- Acne
- Atherosclerosis or the hardening of the arteries.
- Arthritis
- High cholesterol levels
- Skin disease
- Obesity

In a recent episode of the Dr. Oz show, he recommended that people who have slow digestion should take guggul together with their meals. Research shows that guggul helps reduce LDL levels in the body and it also increases HDL levels. Guggulsterones, the antioxidants present in guggul, decreases platelet stickiness and normalizes clotting. It also assists the body in breaking up clots, thus helping prevent strokes as well as heart attacks. Guggul has also been found to be helpful for those suffering from other inflammatory conditions, like osteoarthritis.

It is recommended that people who suffer from high cholesterol should start with a maximum dose of 1200 mg per day. When the LDL level starts to decrease, the dosage can also be decreased. The minimum dose is 300mg daily which can help maintain a low cholesterol level.

Red Rice Yeast

Red rice, or red yeast rice, is a substance that is taken from rice that has been fermented with the yeast, Monascus Purpureus. This has been used in China, as well as other Asian countries for hundreds of years as a medicine. It is also used to color various foods and is also used as a preservative. Red yeast rice has natural ingredients that have been found to help control a person's cholesterol levels. Monacolin K is one of those ingredients. Red yeast rice also contains isoflavones, sterols, and monounsaturated fatty acids that are beneficial for the body.

What is so special about monacolin K? This ingredient was isolated from Red rice yeast and is the active ingredient found in the prescription drug "Mevacor". There have been studies that showed the ability of this supplement to lower the total cholesterol levels, especially that of LDL. The recommended daily dosage for this supplement is still not well-established as of now.

Policosanol

Policosanol is another natural product that is taken from the coating of sugar cane (the waxy part). This is frequently used in to lower cholesterol levels that are high. It has been found to be effective in lowering LDL levels, as well as total cholesterol. This supplement also helps increase the HDL levels. Medical professionals have not discovered what the exact mechanism of action policosanol has in lowering LDL cholesterol. However, it seems that it mimics the mechanism of action of cholesterol-lowering drugs. It has also been found to decrease the stickiness of platelets in the blood. This helps to prevent the formation of clots in blood vessels that are narrowed. A single dose of 5-10 milligrams a day is said to help reduce the total cholesterol and LDL levels in the body.

Artichoke extract

Artichoke is a well-known plant in which the stem, roots, and leaves are used to create extracts. The extract is used to help stimulate the flow of bile in the liver. This is also said to help reduce heartburn symptoms, as well as alcohol hangovers. Artichoke extract has also been found to be beneficial for those who suffer from high cholesterol levels in the blood.

Omega 3 Fish Oil

Omega-3 fatty acids have been found to help reduce one's blood pressure, as well as decrease the risk of developing clots in the blood. The Omega-3 fatty acid known as docosahexaenoic acid (DHA) has also been found to influence proper brain function. DHA is found in high concentration in the gray matter of the brain. DHA is instrumental in the function of cell membranes in the brain and is very important for the normal transmission of brain signals. Fish oils can also help make significant changes in the lipid profile, such as the reduction of LDL cholesterol and elevation of HDL cholesterol levels. Omega 3's also helps to steady the rhythm of the heart, making it easier for the blood to flow throughout the body.

Beta-sitosterol

This is a plant sterol that is quite similar to the structure of human cholesterol. This is commonly found in foods like nuts, seeds, and wheat germ, and also found in saw palmetto, and black cumin. Because it shares a similar structure with human cholesterol, beta-sitosterol can have an effect on hormone and cholesterol levels in the body. This is why it has been extracted and purified and made into dietary supplements.

The most potent benefit of taking beta-sitosterol is its ability to reduce the concentration of cholesterol in the blood. It inhibits the absorption of cholesterol from one's diet in the intestines. This could then help decrease the levels of LDL in the body.

Vitamin B3 (Niacin)

Niacin is a B vitamin that has long been in the picture in terms of improving one's HDL cholesterol, which helps to sweep up the LDL in the blood. It has been used to increase HDL by up to 15-35%. Vitamin B3 also helps to lower the triglyceride levels in the body.

Soluble Fiber

There are two types of fiber from the food that you eat: insoluble and soluble fiber. Soluble fiber is the type that can be dissolved in water. It forms a consistency that is gel-like when it is in the digestive tract. In terms of heart health, soluble fiber seems to be the only one that will give you benefits, especially in lowering your cholesterol levels. It has been found in studies that consuming 10-25 grams of soluble fiber daily can help lower your cholesterol level by 18%. You can get soluble fiber from a variety of foods, such as legumes, fruits, whole grains, and many more.

Garlic extract

Garlic has long been used as a medicinal drug by ancient civilizations. It has been found to help lower total cholesterol, LDL, and triglyceride levels. 900 milligrams of garlic extract daily has been found to help achieve optimal results with your cholesterol.

Ground flaxseed

Ground flaxseed works better than whole flaxseed because it is easier to digest in the body. There is also the possibility that whole flaxseed could simply pass in the intestine without getting digested, which then means you will not be able to receive the benefits. Flaxseed is high in omega-3 fatty acids and fiber, plus phytochemicals (lignans). Every tablespoon of ground flaxseed contains approximately 2 grams of polyunsaturated fatty acids (this includes the omega-3), 2 grams of fiber, and only 37 calories.

Flaxseed can lower total blood cholesterol and you're LDLs. It is also capable of increasing your HDLs. It binds with cholesterol found in the intestine and prevents it from getting absorbed by the body. Be sure to take this with plenty of water to prevent getting constipated.

Smoothies to Lower Your Cholesterol

Cholesterol is pretty much found in all animal and human tissue. Your body needs it to function properly, but too much cholesterol, especially LDLs, can accumulate in the body faster than the rate that your body could break it down. A simple change in one's diet plan can help a lot in maintain healthy cholesterol levels as well as improving your overall health. There are tons of recipes that you can find that can help you to manage your cholesterol levels and drinking smoothies has become very popular and a great way to easily ingest beneficial vegetables and fruits into your body. Here are some good smoothie recipes for you to try.

Blueberry-Avocado Smoothie

Blueberries have disease-fighting phytochemicals, and they are also packed with lots of antioxidants. Avocados have monounsaturated fatty acids, which could help you reduce your risk for heart disease. The folic acid and vitamin B6 in avocados also support your heart health and can help to lower cholesterol levels.

Ingredients:

1 cup blueberries, frozen

¼ of an avocado

1 cup of coconut water

Juice from half of a lime

1 serving of non-dairy protein powder or vanilla whey protein

Raw honey, xylitol, or stevia for sweetening

4 ice cubes

Steps:

- Blend blueberries, avocado, lime juice, and coconut water.

- Add the protein powder and ice cubes
- Sweeten the smoothie according to your taste.
- Serve immediately.

Super Chocolate Smoothie with Chia Seeds

Chia seeds and raw cocoa are considered super foods that will help you become healthier and the addition of oats will help lower your cholesterol levels.

Ingredients:

½ cup of Quaker oats, plain

1 cup of almond or coconut milk

1 tablespoon of raw cocoa, organic

1 tablespoon of chia seeds

1 scoop of vanilla protein powder

4 to 6 ice cubes

Steps:

- Blend all of these ingredients together until smooth.

Heart-Smart Smoothie

Yogurt and almond milks potassium and calcium content help bring one's blood pressure down and control one's weight. The flavanols found in the cocoa bean help to promote a robust circulatory system. Almonds have also been found to help decrease LDL and increase HDL.

Ingredients:

½ cup of almond milk

½ cup of non-fat vanilla Greek yogurt

½ banana, ripe

½ cup raspberries, frozen

1 tablespoon of almond butter

1 teaspoon of dark cocoa powder (sweetened)

3 ice cubes

Steps:

- Blend all of these together for a minute or so, until everything is smooth.
- Serve immediately.

Green Smoothie

This is packed with a soluble fiber that can help you lower your cholesterol levels.

Ingredients:

¼ cup of fresh dandelion leaves

2 to 3 cups of fresh pineapple, chopped

1 cup of spinach, chopped

¼ cup of avocado

2 to 3 cups of water

Steps:

- Chop the dandelion leaves first.
- In a blender, mix all of the ingredients together until well-blended.

Orange Smoothie

An antioxidant found in orange juice, hesperidin, is said to improve blood vessel function. It also helps to reduce the risk of a person of suffering from heart disease. Papayas have also been found to help prevent atherosclerosis due to their vitamin C and vitamin E content. Carrots also have significant amounts of antioxidants, which help shield the cardiovascular system from various diseases.

Ingredients:

½ of a banana

½ cup of blueberries

½ cup of red grape juice

½ of a papaya

¼ cup of carrot juice

¼ cup of orange juice

Ice cubes

Steps:

- Place all of the ingredients above in a blender and blend until well-mixed.

The Food You Eat and Cholesterol

The concept of cholesterol frequently enters any discussions involving diet and food intake. Cholesterol is present in all animal cells and is therefore introduced into our systems through food intake.

So what is the relationship of food and cholesterol? The cholesterol levels in the human body are definitely influenced by food intake. Specifically, the kind of food that is consumed by a person can increase or reduce the amount of good and bad cholesterol in his system. On the one hand are foods that have been proven to reduce LDL (low-density lipoprotein) or "bad" cholesterol levels in the body while raising the amounts of HDL (high-density lipoprotein) or "good" cholesterol at the same time. On the other hand are items that when eaten can cause a spike in cholesterol levels.

Foods That Increase Cholesterol Levels

As you probably already realized it is not only what type of food you consume but just as important how much you consume. If you consume excessive amounts of foods that contain cholesterol they can cause the overall cholesterol level in the body to rise. When eaten in moderate amounts, most provide nourishment that the body needs to function properly.

Foods that contribute to an increase in overall cholesterol level are rich in any of these substances: cholesterol, saturated fat, and Trans-fat. Saturated fat is commonly found in animal products and dairy such as cheese, butter, ice cream, and sour cream, among others. It is also present in plant-based products such as coconut milk and various oils (coconut, palm kernel, and palm oil, to name a few examples).

Trans-fats behave similarly to saturated fat in that they also increase LDL cholesterol in the body. Trans-fats can be found naturally in meat and dairy products but only in very small amounts. The synthetic form is more prevalent, as it is present in a wide variety of processed food that makes use of hydrogenated vegetable fat. Here are the most common food products that often contain Trans- fats:

    Salad dressings and dips

    Commercially baked goods (cookies, cakes, doughnuts)

    Chips (potato chips and the like) Margarine

    Candies

    Cereals and energy bars

    Frozen food (such as microwaveable meals, pot pies, and pizzas)

    Soups (soup and noodle cups)

    Spreads

    Packaged mixes (cake/brownie mixes, gravy mixes)

Aside from the items mentioned above, the following items are also high in cholesterol and should therefore be consumed in moderation:

- Processed meat products
- Liver and liver-based products such as pate and foie gras
- Fast food items
- Shellfish

Foods That Lower Cholesterol Levels

Foods that can lower LDL cholesterol and increase HDL cholesterol levels contain any of the following:

- Soluble fiber – found in whole grains such as oatmeal, beans, and various fruits
- Phytoestrogens – present in flaxseed and soy-based products

- Monounsaturated fats – found in olive and coconut oil and in some nuts
- Omega-3 fatty acids – can be obtained from fatty fish such as salmon, mackerel, halibut, and sardines
- Polyunsaturated fatty acids – present in some varieties of nuts

We must not forget that diet also plays a big role in helping you lower your cholesterol levels. It is time that you eat smart and know what foods are best for lowering your cholesterol levels. Here is a list of the best foods that you should stock up on in order to become healthier.

Soy

Soy-based foods are used to replace meat and cheese, as both have been found to contain high levels of saturated fat. The most important dietary change that people have to do is to reduce their intake of the wrong kind of saturated fat. The liver uses this type of fat to create cholesterol, so this means if you eat a lot of foods that have too much saturated fat your body will naturally have an increased level of cholesterol. The isoflavones found in soy foods have been found to help reduce LDLs in the body.

Beans

Beans are actually very rich in fiber, especially when compared with other foods. They are high in soluble fiber, which is good for lowering cholesterol. A cup of beans daily, of any type, can help lower your cholesterol levels as much as 10% in 6 weeks.

Fatty fish

Fatty fish are rich in omega-3 fatty acids, which can help in reducing your blood pressure and lower your risk of forming blood clots. The American Heart Association even recommends eating of at least two servings of fatty fish in a week. Fish is also rich in protein. The highest amounts of omega-3 fatty acids are found in the following fish:

Lake trout

Sardines

Salmon

Mackerel

Herring

Halibut

Albacore tuna

Note: To avoid adding unhealthy fats into these fish, you can bake or grill them.

Avocado

Avocados are a natural source of monounsaturated fats, which help to raise the HDL levels. They also contain a high level of beta-sitosterol, in fact more than any other fruit or vegetable.

Spinach

This vegetable contains significant quantities of lutein, which is a yellow pigment that is found in egg yolks and dark-green leafy veggies. New research says that a half cup of lutein-rich food can help prevent the onset of heart attacks, as the arteries are more resistant to cholesterol invaders that could cause clogging.

Nuts

Nuts like pecans, hazelnuts, walnuts, and almonds contain healthy levels of monounsaturated fats. They also have magnesium, copper, vitamin E, and phytochemicals that are good for the heart. Walnuts in addition to the monounsaturated fat also contain omega-3 fatty acids.

A handful of nuts a day (about 1/4 cup) promote health, can improve glycemic control, lower your risk of heart disease and help prevent a heart attack.

Tea

Whether cold or hot, tea is full of antioxidants. Tea is said to help the blood vessels to relax, thus preventing the formation of blood clots. The flavanoids in tea prevent the oxidation of LDL cholesterol. Oxidation causes the LDL to form plaques on the arterial walls. These antioxidants can even reduce cholesterol and have the potential to lower blood pressure.

Chocolate

Dark or bittersweet chocolate is deemed the best as it has higher levels of antioxidants. Dark or bittersweet chocolate contains up to three times more antioxidants than milk chocolate. These antioxidants help to keep the arteries unclogged. Research has shown that an ounce of dark chocolate a day can help increase good cholesterol in the body and prevent the oxidation of LDLs.

Exercise and Cholesterol

It is a well-known fact that doctors would usually tell their patients to exercise in order to lower their cholesterol levels. Despite this, a lot of researchers are not really sure how exercise lowers the lipid profile, but with the help of various studies, they now have a clearer picture of what is happening in the body when people exercise regularly.

Regular physical activity can have a big impact in cholesterol metabolism. Exercise has been found to trigger the production and the action of some enzymes that help reverse the system used for cholesterol transport. The specific and precise mechanisms are still unclear however; exercise can alter the rates of cholesterol transport, synthesis, and clearance.

In addition to this, exercise can help lower cholesterol because it helps you to maintain or lose weight. When a person is overweight, this could lead to the accumulation of more low-density lipoproteins in the body. There have been numerous studies that have shown how exercise alone can affect the level of cholesterol in the body.

One study has shown how exercise stimulates the enzymes that move LDL from the blood towards the liver. Cholesterol is turned into bile and is then excreted. The more one exercises, the more LDL is expelled by the body. In another study exercise has been found to increase the size of the protein bodies (lipoproteins) that carry cholesterol in the bloodstream. Some of the lipoproteins are small and dense while others are fluffy and big. Exercise appears to increase the size of lipoproteins and has a beneficial impact on HDL levels.

It has not yet been established as to how much exercise is truly needed to help lower one's cholesterol levels. Most public health organizations suggest a minimum of 30 minutes of moderate to vigorous exercise daily like jogging, walking, or biking. However, a study done in 2002 found that more intense types of exercise, like high intensity interval training, have better outcomes in terms of lowering one's cholesterol. Those who do vigorous exercise lowered their cholesterol levels more than those who simply implemented mild or moderate exercise into their lifestyles.

Conclusion

After reading this book you probably have come to the conclusion that the myth perpetrated that cholesterol is a harmful substance which needs to be destroyed is "flawed." We have all bought into a theory with little scientific evidence which is endorsed by drug companies who have a huge stake keeping the myth alive. That huge stake is the loss of millions of dollars. Unfortunately for many, money makes the world go around. Truth, safety and efficacy certainly take second fiddle to the almighty dollar.

Think about the many vital, physiological functions it plays in the body such as the fact that your brain and nervous system are made from cholesterol. Your body uses cholesterol to make all your major hormones, including but not limited to, sex hormones and adrenal hormones. Without cholesterol to aid in the digestive process you would not be able to absorb fat soluble vitamins such as Vitamin A and E. Every cell in your body has a cell membrane which contains cholesterol, and without that cholesterol membrane, no cell in your body could function properly. Cholesterol is so important to your body that your liver produces approximately 2000 milligrams of cholesterol every day. When following a low fat low cholesterol diet, your liver senses the drop in this vital substance and makes up the difference by producing more cholesterol just to make sure you have enough. I can go on all day but the bottom line here is that cholesterol is not the villain that the drug companies, processed food industry, and medical professionals have made it out to be.

You've been victimized by the same propaganda that has misled thousands of other people. You have been convinced that cholesterol is a vicious killer that must be conquered at all costs. It may surprise you to learn that cholesterol is not a terrible demon at all. In fact, cholesterol is an absolutely vital substance; you would become very weak and die without cholesterol, it is that important.

Recommended Reads

Primal Cravings: Your favorite foods, made Paleo by Brandon Keatley

The 100: Count ONLY Sugar Calories and Lose Up to 18 Lbs. in 2 Weeks by Jorge Cruise

VB6: Eat Vegan before 6:00 to Lose Weight and Restore Your Health . . . for Good by Mark Bittman

The DASH Diet Action Plan: Proven to Lower Blood Pressure and Cholesterol without Medication (A DASH Diet Book) by Marla Heller

Other Health Related Books by Joshua Collins

All of Joshua's books are listed on his website http://joshuacollinshealth.com where you can also find book reviews and other health related articles. His books are also available at Amazon in both the kindle section and in paperback.

Coconut Oil Handbook

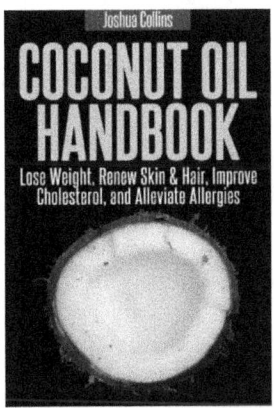

Wheat Free Diet

Medical Disclaimer

This book is intended as a reference guide only and not as a medical manual or medical advice. The sources and information provided in this book are strictly designed to assist you in making informed decisions regarding your overall conditions or problems. Please seek the advice of a qualified medical professional when it comes to making medical decisions. This book, nor the information herein, is intended to replace or substitute any diagnosis, treatment or medication that has been prescribed or recommended by a health care provider, your doctor or a pharmacist. I strongly suggest you check with your medical care provider, pharmacist or doctor and follow their guidelines to create a well-balanced, nutritional diet and before beginning any new exercise, diet program or health related regime. Each person has different needs and requirements, based on their overall health situation. Please consult your physician before starting any new health programs.

Copyright

Cholesterol Myth: The Real Truth about Cholesterol They Don't Want You to Know. Exposing the Global Conspiracy about Statins, Sugar, Supplements and Heart Disease

By Joshua Collins

ISBN 978-0615918266

© Copyright 2013 Joshua Collins

Reproduction or translation of any part of this work beyond that permitted by section 107 or 108 of the 1976 United States Copyright Act without permission of the copyright owner is unlawful. Requests for permission or further information should be addressed to the author.

This publication is designed to provide accurate and authoritative information in regard to the subject matter covered. It is sold the understanding that the publisher is not engaged in rendering legal, accounting, or other professional services. If legal advice or other expert assistance is required, the services of a competent professional person should be sought.

First Published, 2013

Printed in the United States of America

www.ingramcontent.com/pod-product-compliance
Lightning Source LLC
Chambersburg PA
CBHW070107100426
42743CB00012B/2677